## Praise for *Your Stories Look Me in the Eye*

"The heart breaks to get bigger. I want to believe this. But it can break to get smaller. It can break smaller into rage. Break smaller into repression. Or, worse, depression.

Perhaps there is no "bigger" for the heart to break . . . than into poetry.

The fact that heartbroken Palestinian poet Basman Derawi and heartbroken Israeli poet Michal Rubin have both broken into poetry is remarkable. What makes this accomplishment even more remarkable is that they have done so in concert, wounds made words in such a way that the word-scars form two wings of one bird.

And, flapping together, they lift us into common sky."

Lucien Zell is the author of *Tiny Kites* (Dos Madres, 2019) & serves as a peaceworker through his Prague-based foundation Moving Center (www.mclf.eu).

# Your Stories
# Look Me
# in the Eyes

Basman Derawi
Michal Rubin

Fomite
Burlington, VT

ISBN-13: 978-1-967022-20-5
Library of Congress Control Number: 2015956979

Fomite
58 Peru Street
Burlington, VT 05401

09-24c-2025

I dedicate this work to my mother,
my family,
my friends who still fight to survive in Gaza,
my non-Palestinian friends who extended their hearts.

To Eman, Ouda, Essa and every other friend/family I lost.
You will always be alive in me.

To all people whose stories have never been told
nor heard.
*Basman Derawi*

In memory of my father, Chanan Rubin, and of his
commitmentto social justice.
*Michal Rubin*

This collection is a project of co-resistance against the
Israeli occupation of Palestinian land, against apartheid,
and against settler-colonial structures of domination.
We recognize the UN-affirmed inalienable rights of the
Palestinian people, and affirm the right of all peoples to
live in freedom and dignity.

# Contents

# Introduction

From the crushing weight of destroyed homes, hospitals, schools, universities and unmarked graves under concrete rubble in Gaza; from the loss of sons, daughters, fathers, mothers and grandparents to mazes deep underground in an unknown and dark world; from dark Israeli prisons where innocents are held captive, abused and tortured for years, from the land of orphans now missing limbs and surrounded by the stench of corpses preyed on by hungry dogs; from bomb shelters and a false sense of security and safety, from destroyed homes and communities, from a hundred years of dispossession, victimizer and victim, and from the repeated threats of destruction that revive generations of past traumas, still emerging from Nazi mass slaughter. Emerging from generations of inequality and the struggle for liberation, from endless cycles of war and destruction, annihilation and threats of annihilation, the loss of home, land, community and belonging. From two societies living together through years of abuse, loss, mistrust, pain and fear, emerge two individuals who see value in the words of their prophets: "To feed the hungry and to greet with words of peace those you know and those you do not know" and "the work of righteousness shall be peace": Basmam Derawi (Gaza/Egypt) and Michal Rubin (Israel/US) through mistrust, fear, shame, and pain, search for their shared humanity, and decide, in their unique way through poetry, to create and commit to a different reality: one of justice and equality, repair and healing, trust, caring and safety.

Professor David Reisman
Columbia, South Carolina
January, 2025

# Words inside my body

When I hear you say
*I am from Gaza*
I fear my blindness

When I hear you say
*I am from Gaza*
I fear your blindness

When I hear you say
*I am from Gaza*
I  grasp you are alive
to tell more

When I hear you say
*I am from Gaza*
my shame veils my presence
my face my ears my mind are draped
with your story

When I hear you say
*I am from Gaza*
I pale, words inside my body
flutter *I am not bad I am not bad*
I live and I don't know what to say
I think of a book I must write

When I hear you say
*I am from Gaza*
I want to imagine the unimaginable
show me pictures of your street before
and after
name it name your neighbors
before and after

When I hear you say
*I am from Gaza*
I think I must paint the screams I don't hear
and that there isn't enough love
nor enough red paint
and what color to use
for the silence
between cries

*Michael*

# When I hear you say

When I hear you say,
*I am from Israel.*
My blood boils,
I take a deep breath (the only weapon I have, actually).
Whispering to myself, ready for the war.

When I hear you say,
*I am from Israel.*
I don't assume the devil sits
in front of me smirking but…

When I hear you say,
*I am from Israel.*
I expect to see my blood on your hands,
cold and justified.
But you open your mouth,
then no blood is seen.

When I hear you say,
*I am from Israel.*
And you unzip your chest,
handing me your heart.

Same hearts, same humanity.
I breathe again, I almost cry.

3

# A poem

I begin with the end: a poem.
It ends with the smallness of words
a mob of scurrying ants
building a mound

it covers
tombs of possibilities
mass graves of unlived diaries
it covers the dragged sacks
of the displaced

at the edges of the road,
before the poem,
I slipped into the pool of dust
in its depth a door

I don't want to see open
to where the unwritten books
reside and dreams
collect dust

There, the words swarm uselessly
no mounds to cover the brutes
we see in the mirrors

# Displacement

Don't look! Just keep walking.
Corpses at the side of the road.
Can't even confuse the smell with
a rotten dead rat non-deliberately
killed at the side of the road.
Fresh-fallen flesh,
Exposed bones.
The cats are hungry.
They eat one of the corpses.
No, you're not fantasizing,
Nor an actor in a zombie movie.
I see ghosts walking among us.
No, you're not confused.

Don't look to the side

Your neighbor is blindfolded,
On his knee, naked.
His mouth is bleeding.

Raise the white flag.
Don't let your hand shake.
Don't look! Just keep walking.

Stop thinking! Stop thinking!
Don't count your displacements.
Don't look back.

Don't remember the house now.
Don't remember your friends.
Don't cry.
Don't cry.

Just keep walking.

*Basman*

# Who will Grieve the Unmourned?

No one can stop
to leave a flower
on the unburied dead

collect the scattered
unuttered words
nor adorn the broken-off stories

You say *keep walking*

drag the brazenness of death
with your belongings
litter a path with futile protests

You say *Don't stop*

and only the remnant
of your shadow
shelters the unburied

# I was in love with October

In Octobers,
the summer said farewell.
A shivering cold stood at the door.
A young man walked the street of Omar Al Mokhtar.
He turned toward Gaza's sea.
The cold breezes touched his face.
In that moment, October was a poem.

In October,
I taste the freedom of movement.
I walk in a light rain on the streets of Zurich.
I see the high reach of skyscrapers.
I learn the difference between lake and sea,
not from a map in a besieged city.
Mamma Mia! I eat ravioli for the first time.
In this moment, I close my eyes and live forever.

In Octobers,
The olive trees waited for the touch of hands
to turn their harvest into a golden nectar.
Ya Zareef Altool sang while kids played,
then gathered around for oven-fresh Moshkan,
rich in olive oil and spices.
In that moment, no tree in the world was happier.

In October,
The olives die without touch.
The hands in Gaza are amputated.
The kids no longer play.
The singer is assassinated.
The golden nectar no longer flows.
The genocide turns one year old

# October

Someone reports news on the radio / I turn the volume up / all I
hear is inner chorus/ moans crawling on the floor / living forms
wrapping themselves around my feet / I want to free myself from
the grip of the high pitch lament / but I am chained to the caws
which come from so far away / hang on the walls in and out of
picture frames / enter through open windows /without a breeze /
they creep in / lurk and skulk / in October

which returns with a shudder

I mourn the tomorrows under the rubble
I mourn stained clothes on still bodies
I mourn thousands coffins
I mourn unburied limbs
I mourn the unspoken
I mourn the spoken

in October /

I cut up an apple
peel a tangerine
ashamed as I relish
these words
in October /

# Final Diagnosis

*Lung mass*
*CT 11/14/24:*
*Impression:*
*2.1 cm right lower lobe pulmonary nodule suspicious for primary*
*lung cancer.*

*Right lung, needle biopsies,*
*Pulmonary adenocarcinoma.*

I opened my lung to the stories,
to the words, the songs,
to the late night recaps
of rubbled days. I opened

my lung, a guest house
to your yesterday's scraped heart,
to the single boot on the road
missing a sole

and a foot. Objects left
without owners, a community
of shivah stories, pebbles
that were laid on graves,

there in my lung, together
they formed an amalgamated lump,
a nucleus spiculated and nobulated,
with hubris presence,
choking the land of my breath,
as you choke, unable to breathe,
in your taken land.

*Michael*

# In My Taken Land

I open my lungs to
their maximum extension and beyond.
To the last molecules of oxygen
after they burnt the air.
To a story that tells my history.
To a song that tells me I am here.
To a poem tells me why I should be here.

I open my lungs to
their maximum extension and beyond.
Only smoke occupies.
Only the odor of corpses.
Only the stench of worms from
the unhealed opened wounds.
Only the smell of a graveless death.

I open my lungs to
their maximum extension and beyond.
Choked while climbing a mountain before
I remember I am amputee.
Breathless while creating a new skin to cover my fear.

Exhausted by the image of malignant mass of metal
penetrating my hand while overstretching to a new friend.

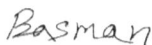

13

## All Naked to You

I am all naked to you, God.
Hold my Jewish friend's lung in my hand, praying.
There is a lump inside.
It doesn't belong here.
Expanding, occupying the space of the little alveoli.

I am all naked to you, God.
carrying all the questions on my head, praying.
All I know is there are no synonyms
in all Almighty's name for the occupation
but cancer.

I am all naked to you, God.
Wearing my heart on my sleeve, praying.
All blood around but can our hearts find a small room for
humanity?
All cancer around but will an escaped breath find a little space
for healing?

# Of lungs and ghosts

A ghost settled in my lung, occupying a new estate.
Some believe lungs are the forefront of defense.
My school history books said everyone was after us
but my lung is occupied

Some believe lungs are the forefront of defense.
I must be an anomaly. [Am I an anomaly?]
but my lung is occupied
it is the ghost of grief that dwells in the lungs, some say.

My lung must be an anomaly, [Am I an anomaly?]
it invites a sister ghost in.
it is the ghost of grief that dwells in the lungs
I am a river of mourning, I spell name after name after name.

A sister ghost is invited in
Gaza and Israel mingle in my occupied lung.
I am a river of mourning, I spell name after name after name,
shattered stories from Gaza City flood my veins.

Gaza and Israel mingle in my occupied lung.
My streets are a river of bones. I pick up skeletons.
Shattered stories from Gaza City flood my veins.
Ghosts have settled in my lung, occupying a new estate.

15

## The New Estate

A poet once said grief is cheap
But who are we without grief?
thousands of ghosts visit me every night
I am a river of mourning; I spell name after name after name.

Don't be scared of the skeleton
Eman came to visit you as her killers left her.
Sisters always take care of younger brothers'
even when the stories can't be complete.

At least, the ghost settled in your lung is
not the child who was under your window,
not the child who didn't have a birth certificate.
You're a river of mourning; you spell name after name after name.

Your estate lied to you.
You ripped the old school history books.
Healing blossoms have grown inside
When you learned heart is the forefront of defense.

Basman

# You Don't Need Your Glasses, Santa

Do you see that black cloud over there, Santa?
There used to be a child from Gaza, waiting for a present.
Waiting to go out with his father to the Unknown Soldier's Square:
To ride the little cars there.
To go to the beach.
To play with the sand and the waves.
To buy a cup of corn.
Then to go home, to sleep
under the sound of the buzzing, hovering warplanes:
the ones the child thought were a part of the sky,
        the sounds of the universe.
Did he tell you about his dreams before he slept?
What were they?
Did he dream about living, growing old?
Or maybe, like other children, he told you that children in Gaza
don't grow old.
You don't need to put on your glasses, Santa.
See that black cloud over there, the one that rose up from the
bombings just a few hours ago?
Under it lie the murdered bodies of the child,
        his father, his mother, and his siblings.
Under it lie the toys, the house,
        and the whole neighborhood.
And an unanswered list of hopes and dreams.

17

# Of holy names

There is Santa, Basman, there is Abraham
and Moses we call on,
cruel invocation as I hear your story,

sitting Shivah for life's brutal humor,
I gather my faith as a bundle of hollow
fires, cold in their disappointing emptiness,

words disperse into the oblivion of death.
You see blind Santa I see dead Moses
or Abraham or holy books,

yours and mine piled on the table,
lifeless. If there was an Abraham, would  there
be a worthy garden to spare from God's wrath,

I sit shiva seven days, months, years, generations,
endless consoling  sink into the sea of Gaza,
swallowed with the bodies of the unburied.

# Why can't I?

Why can't I be Abraham
looking at the face of the sky
for God, for one truth in the world
that wasn't a lie.

Why can't I be Moses
splitting the sea into halves,
saving my people from the new Pharaoh
who once survived.

Why can't I be Santa
delivering a big bag of presents
to the children of Gaza
without being shot or choked under rubble.

Why can't I just sit,
no Shivah, no cruel humor.
No disappointing emptiness, no endless consoling.
No selective God wants me dead.

*Basman*

## Atonement

In the crevices of my days
I am in the prison of my tribe,
crying salt into a drying sea—
the urn of god's tears
for a land Moses promised
to be a river
of milk and honey.

Moses lied.

I speak to it in tongues
I knew not that arise from
the darkness of tunnels and
safe rooms,      arise
from the ashes of burnt homes,
arise from the footprints
of the displaced, arise
from the silenced voices
below ground.

Moses lied.

The crevices of my days hoard
moldy grief
as the eternal light, ignited by Moses,
unmasks raw lamentations
that flood time.

*michal*

# The Ten Commandments

On the Torah tablet,
"You shall not kill"
Wasn't that Yahweh to Moses?

My blood was red too.
My flesh didn't taste sweet.
Didn't you realize that when you killed me?

Sorry to all promises, there was no milk and honey in this land.
There was an olive tree that belonged to my grandfather's land.
There was my grandmother's thobe left in her closet.

On the Torah tablet,
"Keep the Sabbath holy"
Wasn't that Yahweh to Moses?

The 15th of May, 1948 was on the Sabbath.
The holiness of Mankind was assassinated.
The 27th of December, 2008 was on the Sabbath.
The holiness of Mankind choked under the rubble.
The 7th of October was on the Sabbath.
The holiness of Mankind's flesh fell off the bones.
The satanic hungry cats ate it.
On the Torah tablet,
"You shall not murder"

Yahweh told it to Moses.
The IDF soldier told it when he shot the child in the head.
The missing head of a child told it to the world

when he appeared in its dream.

*Basman*

# I met the prophets

I think I was made of questions.
My apologies to the clay.
Every Midnight mass,
a question wakes me up.

Last night, I met the prophets
I asked Jesus, why wouldn't you
let the world save itself?
If it can't, wouldn't it be the one
that deserves to be crucified for its sins?

I turn to Moses
and dare to ask:
How can a man running from
Pharaoh be a Pharaoh himself?

Abraham along with his two sons
came close, Isaac and Ishmael.
I extended my hand to Isaac:
Uncle, your children have been killing me
Since 1948.

Can't cousins sing "This land is your land"
together and mean it instead?
We have the same DNA at the end.
I looked at Abraham and smiled:
Hello Grandpa, let me introduce myself

I am your grandchild, the one
who is Anti-Semitic.

Basman

# There was a promise

Like a shooting star dropping
from through clouds
or a phosphorus bomb
burning the obligations to trust Moses's words
and his inscriptions on imaginary stones

somewhere like a hand grenade the promise came
to shatter the letters that spelled
*he chose us and not others* and the war
between *you must* and *you are free*
arrives at a standstill so I can choose

and I never have
never have to
never have to pretend I believe
because I don't

And you, coming from Gaza,
I look at you, waiting to meet
the *I don't believe* inside you
I think we can meet there
without Moses and Abraham

we can be Jacob and Esau
as they tasted their wisdom
and just look in each other's eyes
we can just look
with a stillness of understanding
and see us, in peace

*Michael*

# My stolen privilege

Overweight guys embrace the winter.
In winter, it acts like a hedge against cold.
On hot summer days, the layer of fat
turns a hellish coat of sticky sweat.

But last January, God's Chosen Police
cast Satan out of heaven.
It grew colder than an avalanche of ice,
even on this terrorist's chilly heart.

Laugh skinny guys; now I hate winter too.

Fat was my privilege, but it has been stolen.
I know it wasn't healthy, but life itself
has not been healthy for me since birth.

Eman was killed last January.
Ouda was killed last January.
The merciful missiles drop cement blankets
over the bodies of my sister's children.

January saw all my nephews off.
Now they are ghosts visiting my frigid nights.

# I am home, surgery was a success

Cancer removed,
a package in the mail,
a card from a Palestinian friend
*there is so much to fight for        be strong*
and I think of rating pain on a scale of 1-10,


a mockery of the truth of 110 Noors,
131 Omars, 439 Ahmeds, Baraas,
Celines or Dimas
whose pain was never
measured
never accounted for


who lived in the unnoticed
world of ether
unheeded in its silence
while my moans grated
on hospital walls
their moans buried beneath
grey rubble

different rooms in the universe,
different gods or kings or rules,
they lived, they died in a land of silence
where names are not allowed to be called out
their bodies under censorship
of millions


I am home,
surgery a success,
a lobe excised,
I cry with my privileged pain
looking at the unused Oxys
in clean plastic jars,
listening to the blatant silence of
the un-named

*Michael*

# Tell The Doctor

Could you recommend a surgeon?
A doctor? A prescription? A remedy?
To remove our cancer.
The cancer that occupied our body,
Our souls, our life.
The cancer that occupied our land.

A similar cancer to the one
you fought before
monsters woke up inside you.
Before God became a land broker.
Before history wiped my existence,
left only you on an empty land.

Tell the doctor,
I am in the metastasis stage.
Is there any chance
cancer doesn't kill me?
Is there any hope for a better death
before living all types of hell?

Why should I die?
Why should I ask to be noticed?
Why don't we have different rooms?
But with equal spaces?
What does it mean Gods exist in our life?

Basman

" The State of Israel so it was declared will promote the development of the country for the benefit of all its inhabitants; will be based on the precepts of liberty, justice, and peace taught by the Hebrew Prophets; will uphold the full social and political equality of all its citizens, without distinction of race, creed, or sex; will guarantee full freedom of conscience, worship, education, and culture; will safeguard the sanctity and inviolability of the shrines and Holy Places of all religions; and will dedicate itself to the principles of the Charter of the United Nations. With trust in Almighty God, we set our hand to this Declaration, at this Session of the Provisional State Council, in the city of Tel Aviv, on this Sabbath eve, the fifth of Iyar, 5708, the fourteenth day of May, 1948"

## Declaration of Independence in Shorthand

I wander through the woven story / knotted stitches upon old declaration / they wormed into dreams / painting flowers / adorning the fables of childhood  / nice words of old professions /


Accordingly
                    I search for truth tellers—
                    they lie in the field
                    their bodies utter
Proclaim
                    words,
                    barren seeds
                    scatter

the State of Israel
>
> on graded rubble,
> it is real, *full and equal,*
> according to our plan,

We appeal

> with our measured words,
> we say *cooperate*
> so we can steal,

we build, we demolish, claim rights, stamp history on a flag, plant,
uproot, we fight, we save, we block, we die, we bury, we sing, we fly,
we dance,
we crush,
we bury,

We call, we appeal, we extend our hand *we offer peace, we offer unity,*

> words burn off the parched
> declarations, and bombs
> rain,
> and bombs
> rain,
> and bombs
> rain
> on appealing bodies

michal

# If I were an Israeli

If I were an Israeli,
I would embrace all my privilege.
Until I stand naked in front of a mirror
and a question comes at me like
a cold breeze of air.

If I were an Israeli,
my blood would boil after October 7th
I swear to destroy all the human animals.
Until I remember the lecture of my American friend
to never answer violence with violence.

If I were an Israeli,
I would want to finish them all.
I would want their flesh to fall from their bone.
Until a whisper knocks me flat out of no where
What if you were a Palestinian?

If I were an Israeli,
I would ask the difficult questions.
Isn't it an occupation?
Do God and history justify it?
What about all the Palestinian hostages?

If I were an Israeli,
I would be in jail for
my refusal of military service.

Not out of sympathy with Palestinians
but because bombing kids, hospitals, churches never feels right.

If I were an Israeli,
I would stutter at first
then build my courage to
dare to tell myself and the world
my old mistakes out loud.

*Basman*

# 1948—A Declaration in Shorthand

According to your plan,
It was an "empty" land.
I was there under the kitchen sink
hiding from your bombs.

You declare,
Your independence but from who?
This was an empty land!
Your democracy but where?
On a stolen land, only Jewish!

The state of Israel,
Shake hands with the white God in November, 1917.
Erase my existence in May, 1948.
Uproot who remains from us in 1967.
Rewrite history in October, 2023.
Now I am the shadow who annoys the heart of civilization.

You appeal for peace
And I am thinking of a piece of bread
A piece I am hungry for now
A piece drenched with the blood of my friend.
What does your peace mean?

## *Be me*, you said

I go there

to live inside the rawness of a strip
search, my breast exposed,
the soldier's eyes jeering at my
nakedness,

I hear scraping words,
Hebrew insults,
I collect their hate,
place it in the belly of my people

to hold and feed
the core of my volcano
as it awaits its time.

At night I lie with the warming
thoughts of vengeance, muddled
     with specks of a dream, maybe,

             a hand

I resist the disturbing specks

             offered a blanket

I hold onto the thoughts

             covering me

I listen to the inner calls

             speaks my language

to fight, maim, kill

                        shame in her eyes

I see,

looking for a place for it

in my story.

*Michael*

# Be me, I said

Did I tell you about my hairy chest that
the soldier ordered me to expose?
He didn't see my heart
even though it beat fast out of my body.

Did I tell you about my penis the soldier
points at and laughs?
It was circumcised too
Didn't he see that?

Did I tell you about my dignity flying with
the Hebrew words freely flying from
the soldiers' mouths like insults?
I wished my fear could fly free too.

I walked naked all along.
Shivered under the claws of cold.
No hands left to offer me blanket. No blanket left in Gaza.
The last one was used as a coffin for a last-minute death.

Basman

# We are keeping your promise

*When asked by a reporter what "total victory" means the prime*
*minister answers with:"It's like you took a glass cup, and hit it with*
*a hammer, now you have shards, then you hit the shards again and*
*again until you're left with [small] squads or individuals — and that's*
*what we're doing."*
*Israel's Prime Minister Binyamin Netanyahu*


Ouda Al Haw, 36
Essa Essa, 36
Eman Derawi, 41
The Kippah is all red.
High five, God! We have finished them all.


Eliaa Abo Holy, 2
Mohaymen Abo Holy, 9
Aser Abo Holy, 14
In Kaddish, I mourn the soldiers.
I cry for my own blood.
But don't worry, God, we will keep killing the Amaleks.


There is no concentration camp,
We block all the gates; the ground, the sea, the air.
There is no blockade.
We control the water, the air, the power, the fuel.
There is no holocaust.
We have killed thousands so far not millions.

Taysir Abo Holy, 43
Mohab Abo Holy, 16
We wiped the whole family from the registry.
We are keeping your promise, God.
The civilized world is keeping your promise too.

Basman

*mik´vah*
*mikvə*
*plural-s*
*: a ritual bath or a bathing place for purification in accordance*
 *with Jewish law*

Merriam-Webster Dictionary

## Mikvah

It is murky water I immerse in
where my body is painted
with howls of buried
words I give in to, becoming
a canvas, a scroll,
unveiling the discarded as
I stretch my body,
extend the skin

to make room
for endless faces, names,
stories, pointing fingers,
footprints.

My body, a prayer scroll,
emerging from the depth of water
consecrated by truth
as if, there is a You
to meet the prayer,
meet the truth, hold
a vigil to a failed
creation, as if there is...

michal

## Ceasefire announcement

Since the 7th of October,
I put my life, even my crying, on hold.
I was living but not alive. Was it real?
My heart was suspended among
the clouds of smoke occupying Gaza's sky.
I have tried but I couldn't.

What will I do when the ceasefire is announced?
How will my heart beat?
Will I realize then the genocide wasn't a nightmare?
Will I realize it was televised, documented?
And there was silence?
Will I realize then this has actually been happening?

When a ceasefire is announced,
I sit at my distant corner, crying,
all the tears I couldn't cry,
I haven't cried.

Singing, all the songs I couldn't sing.

# My fire ceased in grief

I have adopted fully
the ownership of guilt
without a ceasefire /

and the fire of words
ceased to burn inside me
as guilt floods the burning /

as the physical pain mutes
even the whispers
as life goes on 6000 miles away /

winter seeps comfortably
into the cracks in the wall
and I hold you every day in my hand /

your name is woven inside sentences I write
not to you nor to me
I breathe with the ceasing of something /

but the breath brings no relief
so I stop breathing
I just let the grief breathe
fully /

deep breaths /

Michal

# The Gasoline of Humanity

A hundred killed today.
Two white women, probably
mothers discuss the term.
*No, it's not a genocide.*
*They can wipe out them all.*
*They only kill hundreds per day, not thousands.*
In Gaza, a mother weeps for her killed son,
a baby with no milk.
Two bodies stick together;
a father and a daughter.
They're inseparable by love
and the flame that melts even the bones.
After they pour the gasoline of humanity over
the tents of the families and the bodies of the children.
Let's see them die every day, enjoying their skin and bones
Thye look at their pale faces.
Especially the children, those little snakes of Gaza.
Those little snacks of the most moral army
The universe has ever known.

Basman

# Yazan's mother counts his bones

4:30am     South Carolina
Thunderous rain floods, rattles, tangles
letters and words that no longer sprout

unformed words are swallowed
by rabid hunger 6000 miles away,
in Al Shati, the *beach* refugee camp-Gaza

Naeema, the *blessed, contented, the fortunate,*
her name says,

in Gaza

she holds her son, Yazan, the *one who weighs, the determined,*
his name says,

in Gaza

the *blessed* counts with her fingers the 2-year-old bones
of the *one who weighs, the determined one,*
who does not weigh much anymore

Yazan's mother's fingers count his two-year-old bones

two years in the world of bombs
two years on a hungry shaking earth
that swallows bodies ravenously

47

two years under smoke-filled sky
two years of stunted bones
being counted with a mother's fingers

and the "Never Again" is spoken again and again

while Yazan's bones

protrude

michal

**From:** Michal Rubin <מיכלרובין >
**Sent:** Sunday, January 4, 2024 4:05:47 AM
**To:** بسمان الديراوي<basmanderawi >
**Subject:** Re: there?

# Email Harvest

1.
Got your email/
> *Hey Michal are you there?*

I am here, thrashing,
what else can I do?
I am not there,
and you did your homework, the poem
cutting to the core/
> *I would love to hear your thoughts*
> *no deadline,*

lots of dead,
dead stories,
dead words,
dead promises
writing is not enough/
> *But I am totally in. I keep praying, writing.*

I don't pray, I rage,
I tell people about your sister,
your friends, your street
and then they ask.../
> *No, don't think anyone means to kick you out,*

49

*it's about humanity,*
*you show me that.*

you are not sleeping again.


2.

                    *Hey Michal, are you there?*
I am,
on a journey downward into
a river of promises,
chained by stories-

                    *Just take your time*

I walk by that river of history,
the river of kins and crimes,
my keening pierces the air,
mistakes,
must be repaired
not buried/


I am taking a break from my homework


                    *Hey Michal, are you there?*

I like being searched for,
I am totally in, with you/

*let's try*

no deadline
take our time

*strong/*

what else can we do?

*Michal*

**From:** بسمان الديراوي<basmanderawi >
**Sent:** Sunday, January 5, 2024 4:05:47 AM
**To:** Michal Rubin <מיכלרובין >
**Subject:** Re: there?

# Hey Basman, do you ever sleep?

*Hey Basman, are you okay? I am worried.*
*Hey Basman, do you ever asleep?*

It's 6 a.m.
6:15 a.m.
6:30 a.m.
I can't sleep
I hear echoes of explosions.
Did any friend get killed in the explosion?
Was I imagining it? But I hear echoes.

It's 7:30 a.m. now
I am in my bed.
Laughing! I have a bed in this world!

*Hey Basman, I have a cancer in my right lung.*
*I have an occupation in my chest.*

Hey Michal, I am sorry to hear this.
I wish there was no occupation in this world.
Hey Michal, I have finished my homework.

*Basman, you're too fast.*

Hey Michal, your poems are touching.

Hey Michal, this poem is about my friends who got killed.
This is about Eman my sister who got killed with her family in
What Israel called a safe zone.

*Basman, did you tell your family about me?*

I remember you're Israeli!
I have an Israeli friend!
But she is against the genocide.
I have an Israeli friend!
But she is against the occupation.
I have an Israeli friend!
Please, I don't want to make you feel good about yourself.
I have an Israeli friend!
*Basman, but what Hamas did was wrong?*
I am against killing civilians.
But the root problem is the occupation.
*Basman, I totally agree.*
*But Basman, you find a different path?*
I am a poet, my weapon is a poem
But maybe I would throw it at someone
If he comes to kill me.

Michal, what do you think of the resistance?
If you're a Palestinian?

Smiling! *I would be in jail now for joining the resistance.*

*Basman, would it hurt you if a persona poem was done by an Israeli?*

No, it wouldn't. Exposure is an important experience.

> *Hey Basman, let's keep writing.*
> *No deadline.*
> *Let's try.*

Let's keep writing.
What else can we do?

Hey, are you there?

# Afterword

I met Michal accidently in a poetry workshop. When she first said she is from Israel, my blood boiled. I was thinking of quitting the session, especially while this genocidal war on Gaza has been taking place. But directly after the first session, Michal sent me her poem "Words inside my body". Since that moment we have been exchanging poems, thoughts and questions.

This work has taken a lot of courage and moments of hesitation. It's not easy to meet and accept through all what has been happening lately. It's important to clarify this is not a work of normalization. I don't see Israel as a normal state, and there will be no peace under occupation. This work is a poetic dialogue between two persons who share values, seeking justice and see each other's humanity.
*Basman Derawi, January, 2025*

Is it meant to be? You meet someone, a class, a screen. A face from Gaza. Now in Cairo. There is apprehension. There is shame. There is hesitation. And there is a door we both walk though. Basman came with the generosity of acceptance. I wanted him to know that I see him, I hear him, I respect him. I wanted him to know one Israeli who sees the injustice, here with him, face to face, with no justifications, explanations, nor history "lessons". I am grateful for this work, this relationship, this journey.
*Michal Rubin, January, 2025*

# Acknowledgements

Thanks to the editors of the following journals for publishing previous versions of these poems:

"You don't Need your Glasses, Santa"
    *ArabLit*
"when I hear you say", "Words inside my body"
    *Critical Muslim*
"Who will Grieve the Unmourned?", "Yazan's mother counts his bones"
    *Culture Matters*
"I was in Love with October", "My stolen privilege", "Ceasefire announcement"
    *We Are Not Numbers*

# About the Authors

**Basman Aldirawi** (also published as Basman Derawi) is a Palestinian writer and poet. He used to live in Gaza (Basman was in Egypt for advanced Musculoskeletal physiotherapy training course when October 7th events took place and kind of stuck there and he is staying in Egypt now).

He works as a physiotherapist in the Ministry of Health in Gaza. In 2018, he joined the Gaza Poets Society, the first spoken word community in Gaza Strip. He has contributed dozens of stories and poems to many online platforms (We are not numbers, Gaza poet society, Vivamost, Mondoweiss and ArabLit). He is a contributing author in *We Are Not Numbers,* published in Germany in 2019. On behalf of that book, Basman took part in a promotional tour throughout Germany and Switzerland in the same year. He also contributed to an Arabic poetry anthology, *Gaza: Land of Poetry*, in 2021, and the English anthology, *Light in Gaza: Writing Born in Fire*, published in 2022.

**Michal Rubin** was born and raised in Israel and has been living in Columbia, SC for the past 34 years. She is a Psychotherapist, a Cantor and a poet. In her writing she wrestles with the moral dilemmas of the Israeli occupation, and of the continuous war in Gaza, and its devastating impact. She lives with the complexity of having grandparents who were murdered in the Holocaust, and being a member of a nation that continues the oppression and killing of the other. In her most recent work she engages with Palestinian poetry and Palestinian poets, her way of joining the struggle to stop the war, and work towards reaching a just peace. Her poetry was published in numerous journals, and she is the author of a chapbook, *Home Visit* (Cathexis Northwest Press), and two manuscripts, *there are days that I am dead* (Fomite Press) and *And the bones stay dry* (Muddy Ford Press).

Writing a review on social media sites for readers will help the progress of independent publishing. To submit a review, go to the book page on any of the sites and follow the links for reviews. Books from independent presses rely on reader-to-reader communications.

**More poetry from Fomite...**

Kate Magill
  *Roadworthy Creature, Roadworthy Craft*
Tony Magistrale
  *Entanglements*
Gary Mesick
  *General Discharge*
Giorigio Mobili
  *Sunken Boulevards*
Andreas Nolte
  *Mascha: The Poems of Mascha Kaléko*
Sherry Olson
  *Four-Way Stop*
Brett Ortler
  *Lessons of the Dead*
David Polk
  *Drinking the River*
Janice Miller Potter
  *Meanwell*
  *Thoreau's Umbrella*
Philip Ramp
  *Arrivals and Departures*
  *The Melancholy of a Life as the Joy of Living It Slowly Chills*
Joseph D. Reich
  *A Case Study of Werewolves*
  *Connecting the Dots to Shangrila*
  *The Derivation of Cowboys and Indians*
  *The Hole That Runs Through Utopia*
  *The Housing Market*
Kenneth Rosen and Richard Wilson
  *Gomorrah*
Fred Rosenblum
  *Of Our Elaborate Plans*
  *Playing Chicken with an Iron Horse*

*Tramping Solo*
*Vietnumb*
David Schein
  *My Murder and Other Local News*
Harold Schweizer
  *Miriam's Book*
Scott T. Starbuck
  *Carbonfish Blues*
  *Hawk on Wire*
  *Industrial Oz*
Seth Steinzor
  *Among the Lost*
  *Once Was Lost*
  *To Join the Lost*
  *The Dragon of Sassafras Mountain*
Susan Thomas
  *In the Sadness Museum*
  *Silent Acts of Public Indiscretion*
  *The Empty Notebook Interrogates Itself*
Sharon Webster
  *Everyone Lives Here*
  *O Song*
Tony Whedon
  *The Tres Riches Heures*
  *The Falkland Quartet*
Claire Zoghb
  *Dispatches from Everest*

**Dual language poetry**
Vito Bonito/Alison Grimaldi Donahue
  *Soffiata Via/Blown Away*
Antonello Borra
  *Erbario/lapidario*

Antonello Borra/Blossom Kirschenbaum
  *Alfabestiario*
  *AlphaBetaBestiaro*
Antonello Borra/Anis Memon
  *Fabbrica delle idee/The Factory of Ideas*

Alessio Brandolini/Giorgio Mobili
  *Miniature Cities*
Lorenzo Carlucci/Todd Portnowitz
  *Methods*
Jeannette Clariond/Lawrence Schimel
  *Desert Memory*
Silvia Comoglio/Giorgio Mobili
  *Via Crucis*
Tina Escaja/Mark Eisner
  *Caída Libre/Free Fall*
Luigi Fontanella/Giorgio Mobili
  *L'Adolescenza e la notte/Adolescence and Night*
JohannesHösle/Marc Estrin
  *Album aus Dietenbronn/Whatever Befalls*
Aristea Papalexandrou/Philip Ramp
  *Μας προσπερνά/It's Overtaking Us*
Katerina Anghelaki-Rooke/Philip Ramp
  *Losing Appetite for Existence*
Paolo Valesio/Todd Portnowitz
  *La Mezzanotte di Spoleto/Midnight in Spoleto*

www.ingramcontent.com/pod-product-compliance
Lightning Source LLC
Chambersburg PA
CBHW020807130626
46554CB00006B/2324